# One Egg

Louise Spilsbury

Published 2011 by
A&C Black Publishers Ltd.
36 Soho Square, London, W1D 3QY

www.acblack.com

ISBN   HB 978-1-4081-3372-9
          PB 978-1-4081-3373-6

Produced for A&C Black by Calcium. www.calciumcreative.co.uk

Printed and bound in China by C&C Offset Printing Co.

All the internet addresses given in this book were correct at the time of going to press. The author and publishers regret any inconvenience caused if addresses have changed or sites have ceased to exist, but can accept no responsibility for any such changes.

**Acknowledgements**

The publishers would like to thank the following for their kind permission to reproduce their photographs:

**Cover:** Shutterstock
**Pages:** Corbis: Lester V. Bergman 10, Robert Pickett 13, Visuals Unlimited 12; Dreamstime: Aquariagirl1970 5, Chuyu 3, 16, Christian Draghici 7, Vasyl Helevachuk 4, Mike Rogal 17, Saeid Shahin Kiya 14, Rachel Stogner 9, Praveen Upadhyay 18; Photolibrary: Julia Habel 8, Marko König 15, Lother Lenz 19; Shutterstock: Krugloff 20, Mny-Jhee 21, Picsfive 11, Vishnevskiy Vasily 1, 6.

# Contents

# Laying Eggs

An egg is made by a female chicken, called a hen. The egg grows inside the hen's body. Several eggs form inside her body at the same time.

## Cockerel and hen

Male chickens are called cockerels. When a cockerel **mates** with a hen, a **chick** may grow inside each egg. The chick may grow into a hen, which will **lay** her own eggs one day.

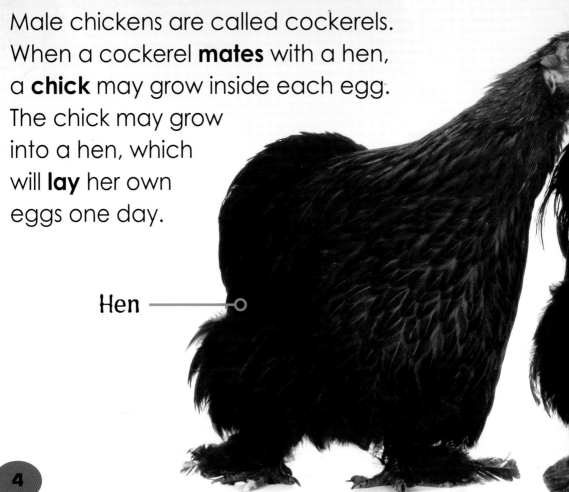

Hen

## Okay to eat

The eggs we eat don't have chicks inside, because the hens that lay them have not mated with a cockerel.

Cockerel

A cockerel has a flap of red skin on its head.

# Keep Laying

A hen lays one egg in her **nest,** then leaves to look for food. She comes back the next day to lay another egg.

## How many in the nest?

A hen lays one egg each day. The hen carries on laying eggs every day until there are about ten eggs in the nest.

Hens only lay eggs in the daytime.

## Don't roll away

Eggs are oval in shape so that they don't roll far. If eggs were round, they might roll out of nests and roll away.

# Keeping Warm

When a hen has laid about ten eggs, she sits on them. She spreads her wings over the eggs to keep them warm.

## Growing inside

The hen's warm body warms the eggs so that chicks start to grow inside them. The hen leaves the eggs only for a short time to search for food and water.

The hen leaves the eggs just once a day.

# Turning the eggs

Hens turn the eggs a few times every day to make sure that the whole of the egg is kept warm.

Egg

# Inside an Egg

A hen's egg is covered by a very hard **shell**. This **protects** the tiny baby chick inside the egg, so that it can grow safely.

## Food and water

The yellow **yolk** inside the egg is food for the chick, and there is also plenty of water inside the egg. The chick uses the food and water to grow bigger and stronger day by day.

The yellow part inside an egg is called the yolk.

## Full of holes

The shell has little holes which let air into the egg so the baby bird can breathe.

Yolk

# Growing

The chick grows quickly inside the egg. Its head starts to grow after one day, then legs and wings start to grow after three days.

## Beak and feathers

After ten days the chick's **beak** hardens and becomes tougher, and its feathers start to grow. After 19 days, the yolk is **absorbed** by the chick and becomes part of its body.

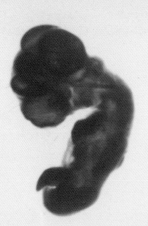

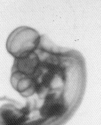 A chick grows inside an egg for three weeks.

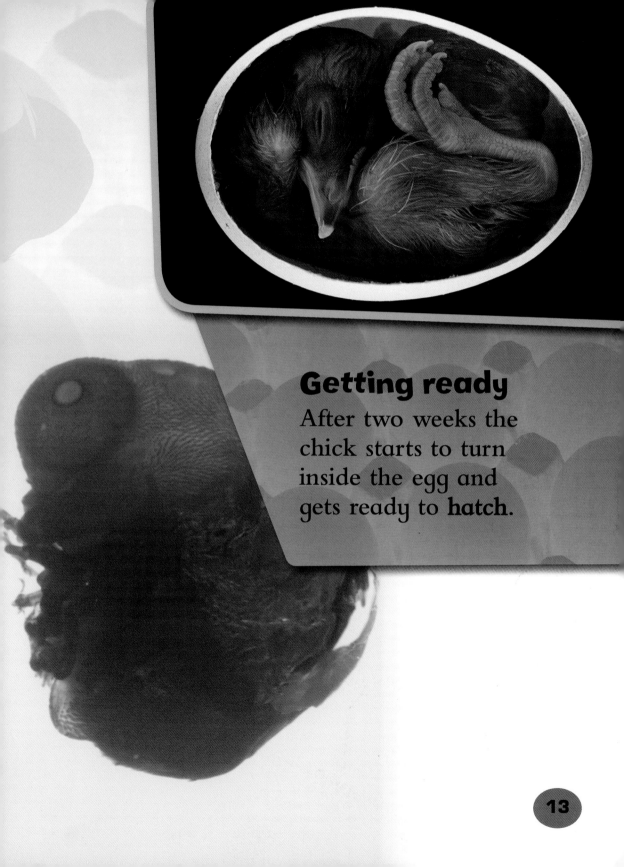

## Getting ready

After two weeks the chick starts to turn inside the egg and gets ready to **hatch**.

# Hatching

A chick starts to squeak when it is ready to hatch. The hen clucks to tell the chick to break out of the egg.

## Breaking out

A chick can take a whole day to hatch out of its egg. The chick **pecks** the shell, but pecking is tiring. The chick rests, then pecks again until the shell starts to crack.

 Hatching is hard work!

## Special tooth

A chick has a lump on the top of its beak called an egg tooth. It helps the chick to break through the shell. The egg tooth then falls off.

Egg tooth

# New Chicks

The eggs hatch one at a time. A hen stays on the nest until she can see that all of her chicks have safely hatched from their eggs.

## Tired and fluffy

The chicks are covered in soft, fluffy feathers that help to keep them warm. Breaking out of the egg takes a lot of energy, so new chicks are tired after hatching.

## Super sleepy

After hatching from their eggs, tired new chicks stay in the nest for the first two days. They need to sleep to **recover** from hatching.

Chicks cuddle up to keep warm.

# Leaving the Nest

The hen takes her chicks for a walk when they are two days old. She shows them where to find water and food.

## No teeth?

Chicks and chickens do not have teeth, so they cannot grind up their food. They pick up **seeds** with their beaks and use their tongues to push the seeds down their throats.

The hen protects her new chicks.

## Staying safe

The hen looks after her chicks until they are two months old. The chicks follow the hen wherever she goes.

Chick

# Growing Up

Chickens walk about and eat seeds and **insects** in the day. They always return to their nests to sleep at night.

## More eggs

A female chick becomes a hen when she is ten months old. She then starts to lay eggs of her own. The chicks that hatch from these eggs will lay eggs one day too!

Chickens peck their food.

## No more eggs

Most hens stop
laying eggs at three
years old, but a
chicken can live
to be ten years old.

# Glossary

**absorbed**  taken in or made part of something

**beak**  hard part that covers a bird's mouth

**chick**  baby bird

**hatch**  when a baby animal breaks out of its shell

**insects**  creatures with six legs and often with wings

**lay**  when an animal pushes eggs out of its body

**mates**  when an female animal joins with a male animal to make new babies

**nest**  safe place where a bird looks after its eggs and chicks

**oval**  long, rounded shape

**pecks**  picks up or taps something with a beak

**protects**  takes care of

**recover**  to get better

**seeds**  parts of a plant from which new plants grow

**shell**  hard outer covering

**yolk**  yellow part inside an egg that feeds a baby

# Further Reading

## Websites

Find out more facts about chickens at:
**www.animalcorner.co.uk/farm/chickens/chicken_about.html**

Read the story of how an egg forms and hatches at:
**http://gets.gc.k12.va.us/elementary/lifecycles/chickens.htm**

## Books

*Eggs and Chicks (Usborne Beginners)*
by Fiona Patchett, Usborne (2006).

*From Egg to Chicken*
*(Young Explorer: How Living Things Grow)*
by Anita Ganeri, Heinemann Library (2006).

*Where Do Chicks Come From?*
*(Let's-Read-And-Find-Out Science: Stage 1)*
by Amy E. Sklansky, HarperCollins (2005).

# Index

24